<u>PREFACE</u>

DESCRIPTION OF THE HISTORY OF <u>BATARD DE MOR</u>

The Mor bastard is a baby born without his mother and father, his mother died during childbirth because of her early pregnancy at the age of sixteen. This child will be baptized by Soukèye who was the childhood friend of his mother Fama.

Before going to the hospital, Fama wrote a letter where she put the name of the future baby and the description of the father who is Mor ...

Fama was the victim of a pregnancy that arose from her relationship with Mor, a relationship that was comparable to the skin of sorrow.

Mor had not wanted to assume his responsibilities, he ended up sneaking away with no regrets.

Soukèye will in turn raise the child with the help of his mother, feed and educate him in good condition. Once grown, the child will in turn find his father, but an unfortunate encounter and wry because the object is a bloodbath ...

Publication: 2018

Category: nonfiction, history

Source: Amazon

Available on: Amazon, Wattpad

CHAPTER 1

If only to live, the man is nothing, he wondered what life is for, why come into the world as if we were dreaming and suddenly, we open our eyes to face our destiny, it does not matter There is nothing gained without a sin, he cried with a cry of fear while his mother slept an eternal sleep, oh! Dear child, he had a great adventure for his life, his way of coming into the world like a loner. Black-eyed, his complexion clear, his skin as sensitive and soft as a mussel, he was born a motherless mother while his father stared at him from a distance through the window of the delivery room and settled on piles absurd questions as for him the child was cursed by the creator, he remained a perplexed moment where the choice was inextinguishable, he prayed without stopping, to ask for forgiveness concerning the decision he was going to undertake.

Mor was barely twenty-four years old, the choice to show the back to the child resonated in his mind like a chorus, he finally conceals his responsibilities and leave him only two drops of tears in front of an ambiguous adventure, to discover his dream, to fulfill it or to relegate it to the background. Without the taste of shame, he compromised without a state of mind the future of this flower. He turned his back slowly, sadly, his face cold, his mind saturated, and advanced towards the exit door like a child walking in numbered steps. Frail Until the silhouette of his face, it was the opportunity to give free rein to the tigress of some men and their disengagement against the lows of life. On leaving the maternity ward, he came across Soukèye, who was the fate of the sixteen-year-old girl; without wanting to be unmasked, he filled his face with both hands while Soukèye rushed to hear the news, his eyes looked, but his mind was elsewhere, the adrenaline was rising, and every beat of his heart was so keen that illuminated, each of whose whales exerted an electric shock that made his body shudder.

In the middle of the night, it was a moment when the conscience drowned and tortured itself with binding questions.

She called the midwife she met:

-Please, Madam, excuse me, I'm looking for Fama. Where is she?

-who are you? Go wait there!

- please, Madam, I am her friend, I must see her.

- hey, sit down, I do my job.

<u>CHAPTER 2</u>

More than an hour of patience, Soukèye had enough, she looked at her out of the corner of her eye to say:

-ah! foolish that you are, instead of healing a patient, you accompany her to her grave with thorns in the coffin; instead of encouraging us, you degrade us with your ignoble behavior; and who am I to apprehend? I was wrong, you are not worthy to wear the white coat.

but you allow yourself to underestimate us thus? I'll tell you something, your friend has learned her lesson.

But what did she mean? In the end, not everyone knew exactly how the famous Fama had made her last sighs, and for what reason. According to the assistant, it was because of the early pregnancy. But in reality, her medications had been stolen and then the midwife Touré was the main culprit in this tragedy.

Habit is second nature, and it cannot wait long without discovering itself; reason why; responsible midwives are needed for patients who are suffering in hospitals. It was a sickening affair between Touré and Fama. Headaches that annoyed him, buzzing, and eyes began to drown in the ocean of the intelligible world. But Fama had opposed a categorical refusal, all this scene had happened in the sandstones of Touré; Considering her a nuisance, she had been sent to the back of the delivery room to bed number six, so that she would not bother anyone. It was from there that serious things had begun; his tension rose to seventeen. After a while, she struggled with death because she was unaided and had trouble picking up her phone to alert her gynecologist, who had immediately called again. When Soukèye had crossed the woman who had despised her, two days ago she was surprised.

but what kind of midwife's working in this maternity ward?

Fama had undergone no treatment, and especially ultrasound, which was indispensable. And this is malice, it ends in the impasse. They then stole her medicine; the room was a closed room to the public.

In Senegal, there was a complex to put the right women in the right place. Immediately another midwife left room three and asked what was going on; Soukèye arose with a disturbing air:

-Madame, I'm looking for Fama, she's about sixteen, I saw her letter in my room and I knew it was not right.

-follow me; please.

Soukèye wondered about Fama's health from a corner; the midwife had looked at her with a desolate face, her eyes wrapped in tears, and whispered, "I'm sorry but only the child is alive."

Soukèye felt guilty, she shouted loudly:

-No, it's not possible, my friend did not leave.

 Lying in bed, nature rocked Fama warmly, her heart was steady, her body cold, the young Fama was napping.

Touré was still unaware that every girl, rich or poor, devoted or loving, virtuous or unworthy to be a mother, is forever the child of someone, and every mother is from another. A good woman is supposed to love her fellow beings even if others suffer from it, bleed, cry, languish, tremble; she must attach her loincloth, devote herself to serve her, protect her, defend her, for, whatever the circumstances, she has formed us from her pulpit, filled with her heart, illuminated by her soul. She gives birth to everything. We are in a dull, gloomy and monotonous world where everyone is free to fulfill his mission or to betray it.

<u>CHAPTER 3</u>

Two days later, the child, stripped of joy, caress, maternal and paternal love, remained in the hands of Soukèye. The rumors annoyed her, he emanated a lack of friendship in her, her face fluctuated like a sorrowful grief, she spent all her time watching the little girl who had not been immersed in the water until then. She dreamed Fama's face, described her body, her looks, her smiles that spoke of eternity, nostalgia replaced the void. Her mother could not help asking herself questions:

Who is responsible for such barbarism?

- who gave sentimental peniaphobia to my little girl? You do not deserve this evanescence of courage, be strong, keep there like your son, his look reminds me of your two months, oh! How beautiful he is!

Death gives meaning to life, it's one of the most enigmatic things. The rendered soul of a being dear to us must allow a reorientation to common sense.

 In his green bed, the religious men led him to a dark, dry, isolated and wry hole. Surrounded by rains of tears, she was dressed with seven meters of white percale while she smiled as a sick child smiled. She was accompanied by four big fellows who each clung to a wrist of the coffin and sang verses of Koran:

- "Allah-Allah" ...

 These beautiful words of compassion and virtue led her peacefully to the eternal world. It was a moment when only the value remained there, the report was global, Fama was gone forever. The lyres, the density sensations and death touched the hearts and minds as a divine message that through its description, insinuated that no one is safe in his shelter. Death comes alone, takes alone, brings alone the source of life of whoever claims that life is eternal.

 Worried and tormented, her sting had marked her, her skin hard and consistent as an anesthetized to whom, the body did not feel any bodily pain, she resisted all pinching, her heart exhausted, the red eyes were immersed in an ocean where prevailed drops of water that did not linger over the course of his face. Her tears mixed with anger that emanated from her heart, the young

Soukèye was struggling to recover. She contemplated the horizon with questions to her creator:

-Oh my God! The Almighty, the merciful, what have I done to deserve this burden? So much suffering, so much sorrow, in spite of everything, I continue to believe in you. So many submissions, so many confidences, ah! I brought you my veneration, I brought you my compassion. Oh my God! I am suffering; I am cold in the sun, I am hot in the middle of the night, I do not taste the taste of life, I do not feel the smell of spring, I burn myself with hate, I drown myself with tears, I whine; My dear Fama comes to you, accompany her to the place of eternal happiness and delight.

CHAPTER 4

After more than five nights of incurable darkness, the time had come to baptize the child, all the imams of his entourage had refused to perform this task, but by chance, Imam Diallo had reversed his decision because of the pain that this family had endured.

Dressed in long boubou and very ample, rosary in hand, Diallo walked slowly towards the villa of Soukèye. Well received, he was not unaware that this ceremony should be done in discretion.

Without Mor's presence, Soukèye said the name she gave to the child: Malèye; the sheep was slaughtered by a scholar who proclaimed this name aloud. In front of the help of Soukèye's parents and her friends who met on this occasion, her mother cut the child's hair: her friend who wanted to have children washed with the water that had been used for haircutting put the baby on his back under a white turban, circling the courtyard three times with a bow, a saber and a schoolboy slate in his hands.

No love of the world can replace that which lies with the mother; a strong feeling, an unlimited compassion, the child feels king with his mother and warrior with his father.

A mother is not going out of motherhood with a child, she is the guardian and the normal educator of children, but what would a child without assistance, his mother? What would it be without the father?

Mor felt lonely, even though his decision he was torturing himself with doubts. He looked at the sky, but his crystalline lens only reflected guilt, he did not even know who his son was. Malèye, in the arms of Soukèye, did not feel the wind of the ball, the one who did not caress the heart, but scraped it, the one who made the scar a wound; all his happiness succeeded in persevering the drowned thoughts of Soukèye. Coming from a wealthy family, Mor had all the goods in the world at his disposal.

With a simple snap of his fingers, his father, rich, honorable and respectful, did not hesitate to satisfy him. He loved her with paternal, boundless and consistent love; but this son had a double face; the one he brought to the house and the one he preached in the streets. A young smoker, drinker, and wry; Mor with black lips, red eyes and a cold face; his mother and his very old father did not know the true face of their son, a young man with opposite faces, he concealed his face so obscure and mean of his likelihood.

He took daily tobacco, without realizing it, the latter reduced his life expectancy barely ten years and reduced the quality of his life by sleep disorders. Tobacco had a psychic hold on him. He relieved him, which forced him to take it to avoid discomfort, remorse and burdens. Smoking created in him a powerful psychological dependence; every time he took a puff, he unconsciously associated the well-being brought by this puff with what he was living at that moment. Regardless of his difficulties, the cigarette made him feel good. This phenomenon pushed him to continue to use tobacco to feel the same well-being. His father, a cigarette lover, did not blame himself for seeing Mor consume tobacco, but for seeing him take his own when needed.

Beside him, Soukèye whispered in Malèye's ear the sweet and pleasant words of Mecano like a mother rocking her boy.

you want to be a mother, you do not find the love that answers your prayer. Tell me money moon, you who have no arms, how to rock the child ...

<u>CHAPTER 5</u>

Five years later, Mor's father was still suffering from lung cancer due to the excess of cigarettes, he knew that he did not have much time to live, his doctor insinuated that it would be useless to leave the cigarette because it was too late. Black as coal, his lungs let go little by little, he coughed like an asthmatic during the summer season; pale, faded skin; old Thiam was suffering; he regretted having contemplated smoke throughout his life, but he continued to use it because, he was not unaware that his end was near.

In the bed of the living room, surrounded by all the members of his family, the old Thiam asked for the elder's presence. Mor was biting his fingers, crawling towards his father.

He was shaking, his body was shivering, his heart was throbbing, he seemed to be in the grip of an inner strength. Squatting in front of his father, he dared not look him in the eyes.

-my son!

-yes father!

I will soon leave this world. But one thing; if your life was a movie, would you like to watch it in the living room with your parents?

Oh, my Father! I have long sought to contain the flame in my heart, but it is bigger. Passions are fatal. I do not know where to begin, I do not know if I deserve to live.

Everyone was waiting for the arrival of help, barely three hours of waiting, the ambulance lingered to come, the old Thiam could not resist his internal pain, despite everything, he gave advice to Mor.

-my son!

-yes father!

Do not joke with your faith, have God as a companion, never forget that there is life, because there is death. Oh! You eldest, my destiny is about to end.

 Four hours later, help came when life was in the hands of the creator. Old Thiam had been silent for a moment, his wife could no longer resist this anxiety; drop by drop, tears flowed from all directions.

The assistant opened the eyes of poor Thiam, but he remained in a position of status, his heart continued to beat, he rushed to bring him to the hospital. The doctors surrounded him and each of them gave the best of himself to save the life of old Thiam.

Through the stability of Thiam, Mor had lost hope.

-my son!

-yes father!

Now you, the eldest, you are a father, you are the father, which is why you must be open. I reached the end of my homework, I left you a fortune, all a wealth. On my back, honor me, if I could, I'll be there, just to accompany you, but it's God who decides.

Here are my last confidences, unite for eternity.

Suddenly, the witness who emitted irregular signals showed a horizontal line. A sign of death, Mor had tightly tightened the corpse of old Thiam, who was no longer there; by the side, the doctors tried to appease her. He began to understand the place occupied by a father in his son's heart, he only had in mind to commit suicide for his disengagement, he blamed himself by saying in a low voice:

-Man can be a wolf for the man, in my life, I have never seen a dog stab another. Without mercy, we lose our humanity. It is high time that I find my son.

<u>CHAPTER 6</u>

 Mor decided to take the right path by trying to turn his page. He had learned a lot from the death of his father, he stopped smoking to avoid cancer because he was not unaware that we do not smoke but it is she who smokes us. After the burial of old Thiam, Mor was still worried and blocked about the housing of his real bastard. He was constantly wondering if his son was alive, he had not seen him since he had abandoned him, his only wish was that he be alive.

-I am sorry!

-why this choice?

- what should I do after five years of abandonment?

Mor had never heard from his son, he was going to find a famous marabout who could guide him to his boy's path. He will visit Seye, a great seer of Toll Diaz, to meet them, he astonished him by swaying his name, the name of his father, and insinuated that his son was his death. Mor did not believe a word, what interested him was to know the situation of his son: if he was alive or in heaven. He got up abruptly to go home as if he was walking on embers.

 He began to realize the importance of the words of his father who insinuated that man must always seek to make the virtue amiable, the odious vice and ridiculous salient. In broad daylight, Mor had the taste of shame. He visited all the seers that people suggested he should see, but the answer was genuine; the death...

 He had no trace of his son, he was starting to sleep with a clear conscience, his only handicap was the lack of excitement. He got angry every now and then, shaking his head like a madman covering himself with the sun. But Soukèye wanted only one thing: to enroll little Malèye in the religious education center where the Koran was taught, because every time the boy saw his friends come down from the daara of Imam Diallo, he petted them with tears of want to do the benches. Wanting only the happiness of the child, she took him to register so that he could have a glimpse of the Holy Quran with his friends. Every day she accompanied him to the door, and on the way down, she came back to get it. Malèye was very happy, ambitious, dedicated and bold during her debut. But barely a week of learning, the idea of discovering the Koran no longer tempted him.

<u>CHAPTER 7</u>

Two years later, Malèye did not want to stay in the daara any more, she took him to the Diandy Private School to start her career as a student. Very curious, the change of space granted him again envy, because his mistress knew how to touch the heart of a child, embellish it, and open the doors of success. Mor could no longer resist his burdens, he ran the fortune of the pot behind the seers with a desperation like a bull before a scene of bullfighting that only wants to crush the bullfighter while ignoring what awaits him.

He found his home at the heart of a knot of tangled problems. Beautiful, smiling, capable, and innocent, Fama was only a perpetual film for him, the one that stays in memories, in mind, and thoughts; she appeared briefly in her dreams, in her solitude, and disappeared in a second like a shooting star. Mor, no longer able to resist this pressure, resumed his research more thoroughly.

 What is wealth for if the family is not there?

It is far from being the positive power; the happiness of man is in the acceptance of a duty; and not in the pocket or in the wander; on the other hand, it comes from the heart, wealth is the family first.

 Malèye who was comforted by Soukèye; hand in hand, they took the direction of the school together and that daily.

 Honor is not a simple word or a reality visible to the naked eye, but despite everything, Mor began to realize that a simple decision can turn against itself and transform itself in embarrassment. Good ones are not bad to choose from, but hard to satisfy. Too late to better redo maybe, but never too late to do well. Soukèye knew him better than anyone else, but not what he was able to do to endure his childhood friend who ends up with a sum, a loneliness, a fatal end. Fama's letter was about to upset Soukèye, who was gradually meditating on it; every word, every sentence, for her had a meaning.

She was beginning to find the answer to her much-asked question.

-Why Malèye? Where did this name come from in his letter?

-Is it Mor, this rich and smoker I had known so much?

 And little by little, Soukèye had made an incredible discovery, she had remembered that she had met Mor in the hospital where Fama had lost his breath. The person who sneaked ended up describing themselves. While being shocked, Soukèye continued to ask a lot of questions. Hatred dominated him, anger, the urge to take Mor in his arms, this time not to caress him, but to show him how irresponsible he had been.

CHAPTER 8

Malèye continued with an ascending rhythm in the educational field, it emanated in him a desire to progress and to have his dreams in hand. He was far from firm but the kind of person who opened his doors to any intruder. He was well liked by his entourage, and at eighteen he was still living in ignorance. It had never occurred to him, the idea of a quest for his real parents, because, he insinuated that Soukèye was everything for him. A few days later, she decided to open her eyes. In his perception, Soukèye no longer saw the child of two months, but rather, a real man able to handle this situation despite everything. A devoted and bold young intellectual, he was there meditating the world to his philosophy.

 His way of thinking and seeing things was still relevant.

Soukèye did not have the ridiculous pretense of hiding the truth forever. For her, all truth is good to say, no matter the facts and consequences envisaged, nor unexpected. His main reason was that Malèye was preparing the baccalaureate exam. But she was afraid that things would turn out badly and suddenly she closed her eyes at any obstacle and forced herself to reveal the mysterious truth to her.

"My son, it's high time you discovered this. Do not neglect it. In this sheet, you will know for yourself who you are, and who you decide to be.

Without thinking, she put in Malèye's hands, a very old paper, with beautiful writings, and whispered to her in a whisper, "Know that I've always been there for her, and that reciprocally, I'm sorry for you announce it, but ... >>.

Malèye had made a strange reaction, he remained for a moment without a word, he remained in a position of status, stable and worried about what had just fallen in his ears. At these moments, he was without sensation, his look desolate, he breathed the burden, the effect of burden dominated him. And for him, it was all a dream.

A letter, not just any, but of paramount importance that had pushed Soukèye to keep it preciously since the death of Fama. She still thought about the despicable decision made by Mor, who unfortunately chose to live with regret and remorse.

Malèye, with tears in her eyes that were beginning to flow. His heart bombarded, his mind troubled, he was living the impasse ...

CHAPTER 9

Life sometimes shows us a land well decorated by foliage, a harmonious and purely appreciated nature. She is there waiting for your presence to whisper her sweet perfume accompanied by crackling insects; the wind shudders, one does not delay the opportunity to emit a deep inspiration with envy; the beaches, the arts that reflect the magnificence, the oceans, the travels, the family, the movements, the sky embellished by the hatch of a rainbow, the changing weather and the sun that invites you to offer you a bronze that makes the body live. But what about living in a mirage, a total imagination of this attraction, what if this entertainment offered, purely natural, all this beauty, these splendid takes place when you are found behind the cells. Mor was not unaware that a minor is not to touch especially when you are of age. He had sold his shame by the hope of a good life.

How to live before the will that burn? How to extinguish our fire by absence? Life gives only one life, but sometimes it is better to know how to choose, because choice requires a will, a desire to foresee and meditate, but the omission of this prediction only opens your arms for you. to draw in a cul-de-sac.

Mor, always submerged by his mysterious interrogation; life? He wanted to understand life himself. The reason why she is there, for him, each presence has a definite meaning: in the hospital, it will be understood that there is nothing better than health; in prison, it will be seen that liberty is the most precious; in the cemetery, we will realize that life is nothing.

He was walking alone, in the middle of the night, a moment when the noises become horrible; barefoot, his head elsewhere, and alone with nature, he did not miss the opportunity to feel guilty, all of a sudden, a false appearance had appeared to him. He began to walk slowly and slowly, reaching out as if to try to welcome a divine presence.

-Wait, please, stay, Fama, Fama ... do not leave ...

 He began to delude himself with a girl who showed her back, with extraordinary beauty, long, thin; and suddenly, she turned, stared at him with eyes that revive, a fleeting beauty whose eyes had suddenly made him live the impossible, so vivid, this appearance passed a light then the night ...

Mor still in his mirages, he began to shed tears, the body paralyzed, it was a moment when he seemed to have broken bones, a moment when the real world and the unreal were touching and colliding.

 Early in the morning, when the dawn begins to appear, an old man who went to work had found him under a tree sleeping soundly, he looked at him again and again, then, he approached with the intention to give him alms, then stopped beside his feet, for him it was a beggar who had lost faith.

Suddenly, Mor opened his eyes anxiously, he began to rethink Fama, for him, what had happened this mysterious night was a divine message that, through the appearance of Fama, to insinuate that she is in an intelligible world waiting for him to come in his arms.

The old man did not stop to fascinate him ...

"Sir, are you, all right?

Mor's heart was pounding, he looked at the sky, the ground ... and he answered the old man.

- loneliness my heart, life my enemy, suffering my mind ...

He shouted loudly.

-OH! My God, I live on fire, I sweat fire, I drink nothingness, I sleep in emptiness ...

The old man was a little disoriented in Mor's tone, which exteriorized his painful and fertile sensation. He sat down and put his hand on Mor's shoulders.

- Sir, said the old man gently, I do not know where you come from, I do not know who you are, but one thing to advise you, life is precious, as long as there is life never lose your consciousness your faith, have hope. Smile life and she will smile at you, flee life, she will flee you.

Mor rose slowly with a desolate air and headed for the infinite in the hope of finding his son.

-no! I cannot do more ...

Mor always in the same accent.

loneliness, loneliness, ... I'm going to search every corner of space, the mountains, the forests, the countryside, the cities, I do not know where you're going, I do not know where I'm going, but I will find you my blood.

CHAPTER 10

Malay, when he had discovered the truth, began to feel guilty in front of Soukèye.

"Mother, I am at the origin of the death of my true mother; she had exchanged her own life for mine, Oh! What a sacrifice! Against a child she has never seen smiling, a child who never knew him, I would have wanted to spy on him, spend the winter in his arms and summer under his eyes, say it how much it awakens my enthusiasm, to say that I do not need to know her to love her, but simply, to feel the gift of her heart. Ah! Bravery, where blood calls blood, life calls death, where error is made, man challenges destiny, but, the love of a mother, he is there, untouchable, complete and consistent.

If you could come back among the dead to feel the beating of my heart that reveals phylogeny, touch me, look at me, touch me, make the wind of love shudder, where you are, maybe you can perceive me, but where I live, I can love you.

Malèye could no longer restrain himself, the words came in waves, he could not help but blame himself, torturing himself with restrictive questions that disturbed him. Soukèye always angry with Mor.

- On the one hand, your father did the right thing.

Malèye had been silent for a moment because the answer of Soukèye seemed a little fishy.

-how? Malèye tells him.

you do not know much about my son. If your mother is a victim of this pregnancy, it was not her own will, but ...

-my father? Do not call him my father, be explicit and tell me what really happened.

-I'm going to be direct with you, Mor, I did not know him well, but your mother talked to me about him all the time. One day, she came to see me with tears in her eyes because Mor wanted to marry her, but her parents refused on the pretext that she was only sixteen. What your father could not stand, then, there were bitter and unreflecting arguments between Mor and your mother's parents.

 Malèye began to have shivers in the body, being ashamed to look at

Soukèye with eyes in his eyes, he lowered his head and began to swing from right to left, a disappointing sign. He asked Soukèye what had happened that day.

-This is the day I gave him advice.

Tell me what kind of advice please.

- I want you to forgive me, excuse me Malèye, know that I considered you as my son, you count a lot in my heart ...

-mother, I know, but answer my question please.

I'm sorry, but it was my fault, everything ... everything.

- How's your fault?

She had come crying, very pitiful, and I had said that the fact that her parents refused this marriage does not mean that everything is over, and that she does not lose hope. I had suggested that there is only one way to be with Mor; to bear one's child ...

Malèye did not know what to say, he looked at Soukèye insolently, with a sorry look. Suddenly, he had his head spinning, he expressed his anger.

Is that friendship? Where is the shame you put in me? So, you dissuaded him, my mother Fama ... but how dare you do that? ...

<u>CHAPTER 11</u>

Everyone did not know the past lived by each other, Mor, Soukèye, Malèye; all of them considered themselves guilty. Where there was talk of social stability, old Thiam had sold his soul to the devil. He had joined a sect where the action of cruelty was not omitted, as a pledge of wealth, power, and power. In this sect, the elites granted total success to the members as well as Mor's father. For proof of loyalty to doctrine, sincerity, as well as commitment; each member should show an act of infidelity and unbelief to the religions by sacrifices sometimes cattle, sometimes poultry, but sometimes even worse, human sacrifices of nothing child at all, with each approach of the presidential elections.

Old Thiam had dispelled his true semblance until his death. In looking at him, he seemed pure and respectful, he was well appreciated by his wife Aissatou, one of the rare pearls, a magnificence that could not be more explicit, exceeds the natural beauty, serer calm, attentive and awake; she ran a danger she did not know, but when love is present, he builds his army to fight the impossible with emotional blows that control the heart through attraction, deafness, blindness ...

Thiam made pitiless offerings to increase her power, because her needs exceeded her expectations, her will had gone too far. In his philosophy, will is the monster of the poor, and power is the glory of the rich.

The day that Mor was born, it was supposed to be the result of a mourning, Thiam should pledge to give the life of his son; what he had not been able to accomplish, a decision that had taken him years and years, he ended up giving his life only that of his son.

He had planned everything, his death was not caused by lung cancer due to smoking, but the ambulance who came to take it was in the act and the task should be accomplished at the time of the displacement, and once arrived in the hospital, it is painful agony that awaits him.

Mor was somehow saved by his father, a truth that only Thiam knew. But his life was the skin of sorrow from birth, which he did not know as much.

<u>CHAPTER 12</u>

Mor saw only his father's money, he totally ignored the source. In this kind of sect, Thiam could negotiate the charges, but that, life for life, his choice was strangely difficult to satisfy, but the life of his son was very important to him. He loved her to die, and he had proved it by action. The exchange of Mor's life against his had spared his son, but Mor had not escaped completely from the hand, the powerful sect, the sacrifices of his father was reverberating against him, what he still did not know, all these problems which he was living, crossing bitterly, emanated from the sect. It was a real fate.

 Malèye was about to do his exam, he was so disturbed by the news, stressed and he had a challenge, success.

 Soukèye did not miss the opportunity to support and appease him in spite of everything. She loved him with a maternal love.

  On the seventeenth of July, an ideal time to fulfill one's mission, to be satisfied and to make others radiant, or to take a step back and disappoint others.

 A few days later, Malèye went to take a look at the deliberation. Arrived, it was not the same Malèye, he was very stressed and impatient, for him there was only one step between success and failure. He thought of his entourage, his adoptive parents, his neighbors ...

Mor, still lost, he finally took back his life, the cigarette and the alcohol were again his companion and that in search of happiness, he returned home and took the most beautiful of his cars, the wine in his hands, the excellence on his lips. He took the direction of nowhere. Soul as a Polish, Mor began to remember everything, Fama, his life with her so much refused. Her unforgettable memories, encounters, moments lived with her, arguments and reconciliations; all those moments that spoke of eternity, all this beautiful life, then he remembered his son, whom he was watching from a distance, shouting ... the car began to roll with a speed of madness.

The president of the jury rose with ease, then he took the list of admitted for the recall, all the crowd was impatient of the results, some accompanied by their parent and the others had come alone, the fear dominated everyone, a moment when courage was relegated to the background. The president of the jury began to make his little speech that everyone had to concentrate on, a total silence, once finished, it was time to take action, sounds of distress and fear came from all sides, girls who could not remain on the spot, they kicked their feet against the ground, their hands against their chests as suffocated. The president of the jury began to recall the admitted,

Malèye was luckily out of office and twentieth of the center, once admitted, he could no longer restrain himself, he began to run with uncontrollable speed to announce the good news in Soukèye. Crossing the road, he was jumping with joy, he had ecstasy in him. In short, he passed from happiness to misfortune; lying on the hot tar, the blood flowed without stopping, Malèye was struck by Mor, the report was global, he emitted no sign of life, he was in a sleepy state. So fast, everybody surrounded him ...

Mor had lost control, he got out of his car with intense fear, then loaded Malèye in his car for the direction of the hospital, once arrived, Malèye was brought in emergency, Mor took the phone from Malèye to contact his parents he looked at the last call to announce the bad news, very frightened, he had the body shaking again and again. His appeal fell on

Soukèye, he announced the news directly; the accident. She went to the hospital with bare feet, so scared; Once she arrived, her heart was pounding, she entered with ardor, and then she caught the first doctor he met. This one indicated the emergency room, and she began to take things seriously, in front of the room was Mor waiting for the news as well as the parents to apologize, what he did not know, c was that he was five steps away from his son. Soukèye had found it in front of the door and she went into action.

-Are you the manager?

please listen to me.

-really? If you have something to say, it will be before the judge.

After twenty minutes of communication, the doctor came out and asked the patient's parents. Soukèye began to lose hope, she got up without waiting and tell him that she was his adoptive mother.

he has lost a lot of blood and must act quickly for a transfusion. Are you ready to offer him blood?

Soukèye was far from having a blood group compatible with that of Malèye. Mor got up hopefully, and miraculously they had the same blood groups.

. The doctor had started transfusing. Soukèye asked her name because her portrait told her something she did not know.

-My name is Mor, I lost control and everything happened. -Mor? Soukèye asks him aloud. Gradually, Soukèye began to doubt him, she began to remember the letter. She asked Mor a surprising question. Do not you know a certain Fama by chance? -Fama? His reaction had all said, Soukèye began to tell him about the story of Fama. I think I know this Fama; Mor replied. Mor began to realize that he was dealing with Fama's friend. The long-awaited moment had finally come, Mor's first question was about his son. Soukèye understood that she was dealing with the real Mor, the one who caused Fama's pregnancy and fled from her responsibilities. In the middle of a transfusion, Soukèye gave him a well-worn slap, then a second followed by a third one, and tell him: you, yes! It's you, you're an assassin, know that the one you just hit is your son, the one you left with all your will. Mor was impressed and upset, the moment he had dreamed had finally come, he was ashamed to look at Soukèye who was restrained by security. A few minutes later, Malèye opened his eyes, and turned his head to the right, he stared at the gentleman who was sitting beside him, his head bowed, tears streaming, Mor was no longer in control of the situation, he prayed without stopping afraid that his son will die. - who are you? Malèye tells him. Very surprised, Mor raised his head slowly, he asked him if he was well, he was afraid of losing his son he had sought so much. But Malèye had resumed his question. who are you, why am I here, where am I, sir? You are safe, my son, I am your father. -Mor? Malèye tells him with an impression.

-Yes, my son, I'm here, I'm your father, calm down, everything will be okay, you just had an accident. Malèye was very surprised, this shocking response triggered an excessive release of adrenaline. Then the cardiogram began to accumulate alerts of an increase in heart rate, very worried, Mor called the doctors without delay. Once there Mor was sent back to the outside of the room to try to revive Malèye. They were doing everything they could to save him. He began to agonize, then little by little, the cardiogram emitted only horizontal traces, a sign of death, he could not finally celebrate his success. Once the doctors announced the news to Mor and Soukèye, it was total chaos, cries, tears that flowed from all the senses, it was a moment when life did not have any meaning in the eyes of Mor. He left the hospital and took the direction of the tracks, once there, he lay down on the rails with the slogan: you will not get ahead of me.

AUTHOR'S DESCRIPTION

Written by NDIOUGA SALL: he is of Senegalese origin and was born February 15, 2000 in Guédiawaye, he is much inspired by his environment and his own life where he draws the material of his work.

He wrote his first story entitled **LE BATARD DE MOR** *where he emphasizes the importance of responsibility and in the story, he places a great importance on the question of life and death that appear on the most important questions enigmatic. He criticizes the negligence of midwives, and focuses on the Senegalese culture that begins to lose its value. This story is so appreciated by Wattpad where it was born in 2018 and it saw the success on amazon.*

END